ALL OUR BROWN-SKINNED ANGELS

ALL OUR BROWN-SKINNED ANGELS

Raúl Sánchez

MoonPath Press

Poetry

ISBN 978-1-936657-04-9

Cover art: "Mayan Angel" by Rene Julio, 2006
Center: Egg tempera on chalkboard
Frame: Acrylic on wood

Author photo by Jenny Stewart

Design by Tonya Namura
using Gill Sans and Minion Pro

MoonPath Press is dedicated to publishing the
best poets of the U.S. Pacific Northwest

MoonPath Press
PO Box 1808
Kingston, WA 98346

MoonPathPress@yahoo.com

http://MoonPathPress.com

Acknowledgments

I am deeply grateful to the editors of the publications where these poems previously appeared, many in somewhat different versions:

"Gravity" *The Sylvan Echo.net*
"Minimum Wage" *La Bloga*
"Brown Angels at Work" *La Bloga*
"In Praise of Poets Responding to SB 1070"
   La Bloga
"MEX—I—CAN" *Latino Northwest Magazine,*
   Speaking Desde Las Heridas, and *Gazoobitales.com*
"Mestizo" *Miracle Theatre Anthology by Viva La Word*
"Blessed Is She" *La Bloga*

I especially would like to thank Lana Hechtman Ayers for believing in me and encouraging me to publish my work. This book would not exist without her.

My gratitude to John Burgess for his friendship, collaboration, and advice.

My appreciation to Los Norteños writer's group where some of these poems were created.

My most sincere and heartfelt gratitude to my wife and daughter for putting up with my craziness and giving me space to complete this project.

I also would like to thank Rene Julio for his beautiful multimedia work "Mayan Angel" and to Jenny

Stewart for taking the photographs for the book. I appreciate your creativity and solidarity in this endeavor.

for those who are not here to hold it

for those who are here to read it

Contents

ALL OUR BROWN-SKINNED ANGELS

uno

The last thing one discovers in composing a work is what to put first.

Blaise Pascal
Pensées (1670)

Gravity

A woman next to me asks
are you writing a poem?
Scribbles I say
from all the places
I left behind:
family mysteries
incidents come to mind
toilet paper ripping beyond the notches
social arts delivered on snack trays
my father's business
Uncle Parcel's tips challenged
revenge's mastery
philosophers' teachings
unfamiliar sand tricks
seventy-five degrees longitude
being submerged in holy rivers
anointed *paramahamsas*
above the self, my self
not for herself, itself
half empty whiskey glasses
translated stories five degrees below
the tropic of cancer
scorching sand illuminated
reflecting sunglasses
empty whiskey glasses
no faith in things unknown
findable frequencies of facts
the world a glass full of rain

the world a plane
landing on a tiny runway
the world at my feet
held down by gravity

Minimum Wage

He risked
climbing walls
jumping barbed wire
crossing deserts, mountains
crawling sewage ducts
eluding *la migra*

He almost died, but survived
and made it to the promised
land

He works—
dish washing
table serving
house cleaning
dog walking
car washing
yard working
house keeping

This is his work
his community
his church
his neighborhood
his family
his home

Yet there's border wars
laws that make migrants outlaws

He does what others don't like
He risks his life every day
for the minimum

Brown Angels at Work

Brown angels are everywhere
We observe them mowing lawns
raking, blowing leaves
dangling from tall buildings

washing windows, painting
roofing houses
They are in your kitchens
serving, smiling

They park your cars
Out in all kinds of weather watch
them picking fruits and vegetables
breaking their backs

On freeway ramps we witness them
selling flowers, hub caps
Brown angels are attending church
going to night school, college-bound

These angels don't fly
They walk the same sun-baked
earth that you and I do
sowing seeds

of prosperity deep down
in *this* American soil
This economy's wheels turn
on the axles of immigrant sweat

brown angel sweat
Lately the wheels are stuck
in intimidation's mud
discrimination's muck

If brown angels could fly
hover over fertile fields and cities
of *this* American land they would
perform miracles, *milagros*

Mexico City in Dali's Eyes

unfinished stucco houses
brick and mortar narrow doors
exposed rebar scratching the sky
winding cobblestone streets
too many cars, buses
changing lanes with no warning
pedestrian crossing traffic lanes
suicidal clowns, windshield washers
stop light vendors
traffic cops, corrupt cops
prostitutes, cathedral bells, bars
taco stands, street beggars
sidewalk vendors plastic shoes
melting asphalt
jarras dripping *pulque*
dogs on rooftops barking to the wind

Fernando

His voice a squawky reed
telling long gone stories
of his town
lost in the past

Fernando talks about bridges
and rivers crossed
leaving behind his verdant village
where everybody knew each other's
joy and pain

"Hace mucho frío"
It's too cold here
he mutters into the sound
of the rake and the rustling leaves

Fernando keeps hoping
to wake up in the America
balmy as his passionate dreams
the America others foretold

In Praise of Poets Responding to SB 1070

Behind the great wooden gate
past the threshold
our memories blossom in the open air
under the blue star-spangled sky

Our cultures coalesce
into a tapestry of colors and accents
and flavors— Café con Leche
black and white

Cuba, México, Venezuela, Colombia
Borinquen bella escuchen mi llanto
la patria aquella que se ve de lejos
y se siente cerca

Argentina, Chile, Paraguay
far away yet near, our thoughts
y pensamientos connect
place with state of mind

Our traditions link families
create lasting friendships
Our traditions strengthen bonds
Our voices rise

poets, writers, artists
aligned with ethnic pride
with dignity and respect
love for *la Raza*

We are just another shade of brown
living en el norte, north of Aztlán
United in this land
we are all free Americans

Right Time, Wrong Place

"You have the right to remain silent"
First time I heard the bark
was after being slammed
up against a police car
corner of 5th and Main
trigger-trained, baton-wielding
black uniforms with covered badges
next to the chicken stand
The corner street lamplight
could bear no witness

*"Anything you say can and will
be used against you in a court of law"*
Baton pokes in my sides my ribs
"Spread your legs now!"
Hands up against the door
steel cuffs pinched tight
intimidating rage blasted at me
not knowing what to say
I didn't say anything—
they made me *"respond"*

"You have the right to an attorney"
Only if I knew what to do
I couldn't choose an attorney
nor the drunks, prostitutes
transsexuals, petty thieves
booked into the precinct like me
fingerprinted, strip-searched

latex finger probing private cavity
found nothing—only stench

"If you can not afford an attorney
one will be provided for you"
Benevolence: assigned public defender
who recommends I plead *"Guilty"*
All they found on me—
a box cutting knife
concealed *"weapon"* they said
two year probation
"lucky" it is just a misdemeanor
not a felony
my attorney said

"Do you understand the rights
 I have just read to you?"
Of course not
I've never been arrested
Could you repeat that Mr. officer?
Who's that Miranda guy?
There are no rights on the street—
scare tactics, harsh words
I submitted to it
If I resisted I could've had my head
slammed on concrete

"With these rights in mind
do you wish to speak to me?"
Told the cops I didn't have anything
They pounded me with questions
determined to get me
for something, anything, because
"I looked like the guy they were after"

They inked my fingers black
booked me
with equal injustice for all

Where I'm From
after George Ella Lyon

I am from *cazuelas de barro*
from *mole* and tamales
I am from the restaurant my father owned
My burning mouth remembers

I am from the honeysuckle creeper
the fig tree, jacaranda
whose long-gone limbs I remember
as if they were my own

I am from fiestas and piñatas
from late nights and early mornings
from *chocolate caliente*
I am from *apúrate y callate*
from *Reyes Magos y dulces*

I'm from Victor and Elena
and *más vale tarde que nunca*
I'm from México, *barrio norte*
caldo de hongos
from *paso del norte*
to work the fields
good times, from *familia*

From mother's closet stash
of letters sent and received
her hand embroidered *I Love You's*
I am from learning English in my youth

from hard work
from love
still growing along my family tree

MEX – I – CAN

Be all you can be *"Ese!"*
Shiny shoes, baggy pants, buttoned up shirt
bandana on my head, standing on the corner
Looking   watching   thinking…

Brown skin
"Familia" mixed blood
Mestizo, Chicano, Latino
"Mi tierra", here, there
Over there…

We are here, we have been here
We're not going anywhere *Ese*!

"La línea", jumping, running
towards the *Promised Land*
wet brow, sweat, the hard labor
of dignity and pride

When we work the land
sun, rain, fertile thoughts of freedom
To live, to love, to grow
Cruising life *"bajito y suavecito"*
taking the bumps slooooow and easy

My *"familia"* migrated north before
borders and chainlink fences
feelings, political defenses

green cards, racial profiles
"*Mi familia*" severed…

"*México Lindo, Sacramento adorado
En Tejas te dejo mi corazón mojado*"
A river runs through
your drowning…
our hopes "*y su esperanza*"

American dream, impossible dream
Label me not for I won't
live on dreaming
Stereotyped "in the box"
shut out by prejudice

I am, what you can not see
behind the rags, beyond the skin
color…brown
brown as the earth I'm standing on

What I have, I have earned
with dignity
I have earned your respect
because I am
Mex – I – Can!

Mestizo
Written on Día de la Raza (Columbus Day)

Tall white bearded men
covered in shiny armor
radiant, like the sun ::
deceiving, blinding, abstract ::
pilferers—dirty, lusty disrespectful

Brandishing sword and cross
brandishing words of authority
enslavers of our people

Raza de Bronce
descendents of Quetzalcóatl
descendents of Huitzilopochtli:
fear not
our gods have not abandoned us

Our gods live with us
our traditions
our food
our values

Progress is irrelevant
compared with the atrocities
brought about by
European greed

Great city of Tenochtitlán
great example of Mesoamérica

is buried beneath
their cathedrals and palaces

Mexica pride triumphs
in a revival of ancient medicine
and Nezahualcóyotl's poetry
inspiring all to the ardent fervor
of the mixed blood within us

Desendents
born out of rape
not a pure indian
but pure at heart

Let us take shelter in
Xochipilli, Tonantzín, Tlaloc
and Tezcatlipoca, the God of War
May *Cuitláhuac* and *Cuauhtémoc*
give us strength to fight *por nuestra raza*!

Let us brandish
Nezahualcóyotl's pen
not the sword of Cortez
honoring the innumerable fights won
without weapons

El Árbol de la Noche Triste
proof of Cortez's defeat
his tearful retreat
Never forget the Mexica blood
is spread throughout the land

Sánchez

Blessed cutlass handle shaped like a cross
absolved by the blood of Christ
the Lord behind their shields
christening the land
with their cross on the sand
a new colony now called :: the New Spain

Last name Sánchez passed on by birth
from original rape to this day
History is not fiction
I don't feel like a Sánchez
I feel I belong to the earth, to the temple stones
Aztec, Mayan, Giant Olmec heads
jade masks, golden necklace, quetzal feathers
burning copal, purifying smoke
and the thunderous sound
of the conch shell, blown in ceremonies

to Coatlicue, Quetzalcóatl
Xochipilli, Tezcatlipoca the God of War
Xipe Totec the God of Death
and Mictlantecutli the Lord of the underworld

I belong to ripe corn grown on fertile land
to Popocatépetl and Iztaccihuatl
I am a blend of Otomí and Purepecha

I don't feel like Sánchez when
I walk through museums

I don't feel like Sánchez when
I see my people adopting foreign names
I don't feel like Sánchez when
I see an indigenous face
named *Brittney*

I don't feel like Sánchez when
pride is gone
history gone
eyes, tongues, blood
Mestizo!

I don't feel like Sánchez anymore
I don't want to be Sánchez anymore

I carry the blood of the conquistador
I kept the soldier's language
only one percent
of his blood is in my blood
I cannot change that
but I can change my name ::

I revere the earth, the sun, the wind, the rain
the four directions

I am a man of this earth
my name is Tlaltécatl

26

Back to Aztlán
for Día De la Raza (Columbus Day)

Aztec dancer's headdress
of brightly colored feathers
sways with her rhythmic steps
with *Teponaztle's* beat
a kind of flattery
to the gods

Aztec dancer's smile glistens
fittingly across generations
Ancient rituals unfurl
with fire's luminance
the winds caress
mountains rivers oceans
the winds follow the moon
Metztli back to *Aztlán*

Some monks went back to Spain
some monks stayed in our land
where cathedrals erected
rejected our gods
our valley became theirs

We lived up on San Miguel hills
closer to the mines and mills
extruding silver for the king of Spain

Saint Michael and all the saints
brought to Aztec land

by Spaniards with cutlass crossed hands
slaughtered our religion

European ways replaced Aztec rituals
Like savages they accused us of being
the Spaniards cut the tongues
of our *Nahuatl* speakers
Our sacrifices were for the gods
not without meaning

The invaders raped our mothers
betrayed our brothers
pillaged our cities
took all the gold
but not all our blood
What blood was not spilled
lives on
flows on
the Aztec in us still

All Our Brown-Skinned Angels

No human being
has the right to deprive
others from their freedom

but we live amongst people
who carry stones
instead of hearts

hatred on theirs tongues
These descendants of colonizers'
racist agenda

is always to get rid of those
that don't fit their way of being
Fear and threats are their weapons

laws such as HB 56 and SB 1070
imposed by judges and rulers
to carry out ethnic cleansing

to eradicate from our soil
all our brown-skinned angels
all our brown-skinned angels

Our skin is not dirty
Our language is not obscene
We are not garbage

The sun shines the same

on all people
no matter how they treat us

We will no longer run
from our oppressors
We will not hide

If we must fight
we will defend ourselves
by our united hearts

Our strength is in our blood
in our voice, in our history
We are warriors, *Mexicatiahui*!

dos

It's much more important to write than to be written about.

Gabriel García Márquez
Writers at Work—Sixth Series (1984)

It Is Here Today

Eight-forty-three past meridian
words come raw as rain

No plans to write this tonight

Fresh soup left on stove top
round and round
the night folds in

mind folds out
a thought
many thoughts
not to forget
what must always remain
lively pumping
that blood with *Sabor*!

simple y humilde del
Indio Mexica sangre caliente
con ritmo Teponaztle beat
rhythmic beat

Conch shell blows liberating sound
from evil used in *limpias* back
way back in Old Tenochtitlán

Radio on the night stand
good news, bad news
living in the world

the new world
my world

My savings
my money
my life all getting shorter
closer to the moment

Never mind me
I'm just writing
a poem at eight-fifty-seven

Euphoria

Tonight
I feel like *Huracán Ramírez*
Blue Demon, Lucha Libre champions
slamming *rudos* at the *Coliseo*

I live for a *noche de tango*
and red wine, vino *tinto*
singing with Carlos Gardel
milongas with versos
de Neruda whispered
in the ear *de la mujer*
the woman I love
que yo más quiero

I feel like a kid skipping
down rain soaked sidewalks
I feel like sitting on white porch steps
cigar in one hand
Cuban rum in the other

I don't care about piñatas dangling
sticks batting the air
no candy tonight
All the children
safe in bed

Running scared from the sacred
called and recalled
I am alone at last
tonight

Cliff's Edge

You and I hold hands by cliff's edge
watch the ships sail
with the crossing breeze
admire the ancient archipelago

If tomorrow we lose our sight
become completely blind
we could stand still by the edge
of this cliff
for the *wind* will show us how

Hear me now—
you and I are born from such mysteries

In the Dark

To be in the dark
to hear our hearts beat
to feel the rushing blood in our veins
to hear our lungs fill
to touch each other

Your skin
an unexplored landscape
an unwritten poem

How many stories can I pull
out of your navel
when I'm deep
in the crevasse of your love?

I cannot see
the prose in your eyes
but I can hear
music in your breath

No need to hurry

These are ways to invest ourselves
before the light comes

Until then
we can wear our joy
in the dark

Morning Reckoning

If I were to measure
how high the sun is
at six-thirty-six
I would say it is about
one hundred feet
from the top
of the pine tree
only a cotton cloud above

Salsa Weather Report

88 degrees in Miami
92 in Santo Domingo
Yuma City 93
today, 85 in Honolulu
and Waikiki

Us?
damp
with
40
degree
basements

I play salsa music
drink *mojitos* and
I am in balmy San Juan

A jacuzzi's turbid waters
to compare with San Diego
and La Joya beaches
bikini weather by the shore

I turn the thermostat up
disrobe down to my shorts
and play Jimmy Buffet's
"Margaritaville"
scuba-diving-Key-West-weather
while I drink *Papa Dobles*
Hemingway's favorite

I live in Seattle so
I clean the moss off my shoes
fling the slugs off my porch!

Every Dress a *Decisión*
after Elizabeth Austen

My older sister could never
ever decide what to wear
on Friday and Saturday nights

My parents told her *too short, too tight*
what that meant I didn't understand
all I know is that my older sister

went away wearing her platform shoes
and skin-tight skirts every time
she could sneak out

after my parents went to bed
and I fell asleep
while watching Superman

Lo Que Importa
after "Una brújula" by Jorge Luis Borges
with input from John Burgess, Punk Poem #49

Here is the matter:
all things we see in the world
we must refer to in language
by words with strange names

Atoms are the matter we see
We give names:
stainless steel
sand, stones and paint
And these same things
have different names:

"acero inoxidable, arena, piedras y pintura"
"rostfrei stahl, oder sand, felsen und schminke"

What we make with these things
how we use these things is relevant
edifying, constructive

We remove the sand and stones
erect steel towers
adorn the towers
with stainless steel
cover them with paint
add glass windows
made out of sand

We make guns from steel and bullets with lead

We make canons to blast
somebody else's painted towers
back to sand and rocks

What *matters* is what we do with all things

Breath

At day's end we try to remain bright
speak colorfully, for words
are like the clothes we wear—
we wear them on our tongues

Dandelion

My daughter and I wrote a poem last night
We picked ideas and objects to write about
We mixed them up
in a salad bowl
carefully tossed

We picked funny words
to make happy sounds
We added, repeated, deleted

We laughed and fell to our toes
pretended to be dandelions
waiting for the wind
to shake us up

We acted like daffodils
and tulips soaked in rain
We opened ourselves in the morning
and closed our petals
when the sun ran away

We agreed that our poem
should be like a dandelion
so when shared with others
the words will float to the ears
of those who listen

Carried by our breath
like the dandelions fuzzes

in the breeze
and so, my daughter and I
wrote a poem last night

Flower Girl

My daughter decorates the driveway
with a carpet of flowers. She cuts pieris japonica
purple and white grape hyacinth
viburnum leaves and ligustrum buds until
summertime roses come into bloom

In India, creating a carpet of flowers
is a custom to welcome visitors

To me it is a sign of something else—
that my daughter had lived previous lifetimes
How else can I explain?

Her kindness, her love for others, her
warm welcome to our blue house

My daughter has no wings
but she is an angel with brown skin

Ten Years Gone

in memory of my son,
Késhava Kumara Sánchez 9-3-1987 to 7-9-2000

I could not
teach my son
how to be a man

he'll always
be
a boy

standing by the water's edge
smiling
in that photograph

I speak his name
I speak his name
in silence

Family Tree

Long, long ago my father and I
planted a maple tree
in the backyard
of the old blue house

One misty, Monday morning
he held my hand and walked
the lengthy backyard
to find the spot, the perfect spot
for the tree to grow
to unravel its branches

The years passed as I grew up along
with the young seedling
At age eight, the tree had one
strong branch where dad hung
the swing

the same swing from which
I used to look up to the sky
and chase clouds, chase the wind
with every pump of my feet

The tree got bigger than expected
the trunk thicker
as my father grew older and weaker

Many more branches sprouted
More children including my own
have swung from the faithful maple

Sheltered under its shade
we sing and dance
remembering past seasons
We plant new seedlings
from our family tree

My father is gone now
The maple tree remains
a paragon of father's
immortal love

My Father Was a Bracero

I know this:
my father was a Bracero
I hold his contract

yellow paper full
of restrictions
and prohibitions

his pay stub
not enough to survive
I wonder what he had to endure

I wonder if the DDT sprayed
on his face over the years
contributed to his ailments—

diabetes, asthma, the cerebral embolism
that blinded him
Laying railroad tracks

expanding commerce routes
from Texas, Alabama
Mississippi, Louisiana

My father's dried sweat merged
with that soil
under a burning sun

another nail on the ties
He went back to *Mexico-Tenochtitlán*
started a restaurant

so he could send me
to a private American school
He wanted me to learn

their language
to live way north
across the border line

He didn't want me to live
by my strong back, my strong arms
but by my words

The Cremation of Doña Elena
for my mother

She rose to the heavens
her flesh and bones
evaporated in the afternoon

Smoke filtered and lifted up
in shimmering rings
embraces for those she loved

Tonight I inhale deeply
fill my lungs
with

what still remains
in the air
of my mother's essence

Blessed Is She

Our Lady of Guadalupe
Our Revered Mother
Holiest Virgin
Tonantzin Cemicac Ichpochtzintli

I see her with folded hands
behind glass and neon lights
above the Mexican flag
tattooed on men's backs

Her image colored by children's hands
messages on *papel de estraza*
on window stickers, *retablos*
on top of cars and trucks

Her image dangling from rear view mirrors
adorned with colorful lights
to whom immigrants pray
to get them safely to the other side

Praying, waiting for her blessing
on old ladies' hand rosaries
I see her on the back of bullfighters' capes
embroidered with golden thread

Moros and Cristianos, Aztec dancers
drum-beat-rhythmic *teponztle*
conch-shell sounds the *Concheros* play
copal lingers to the shrine

Pilgrimages to the holy shrine
covered under *rebozos, sombreros*
the faithful from all over the valley
of Anáhuac, waving pennants

Beyond Zacapoaxtla
bearing her image on their foreheads
twelve candles carried along the way
to the hill *El Cerrito* to pay *La Manda*

Red roses fragrant roses at her feet
her blessing shines on the faithful
who visit her house pinning *Milagritos*
on the Hill of Tepeyac

"Ca oncan niquincaquiliz in inchoquiz
in intlaocol, inic nicyectiliz nicpatiz in ixquich
nepapan innetoliniliz, intonehuiz, inchichinaquiliz"

"There I will listen to their lament
their sorrow, to remedy, to alleviate
all their needs, their miseries, their pain"

I Heard the News

I heard the news
Sathya Sai Baba

is dead

the Dalai Lama
is ready to die

My guru has been dead
for years

Some day I will die

Yes I will die and
when I die, think of me
as the guy who bowed down to things
greater than himself
uttered those names in awe
dutiful
bestowed in humility
paid reverence with folded hands

May your poems and prayers
lift me above these earthy fields
move me beyond ethereal realms

Come what may
let my last breath be a poem

Notes

The Aztec word México means "In the navel of the Moon" and is pronounced Meshico.

"apúrate y callate" \ shut up and hurry

"bajito y suavecito" \ low and easy

"barrio norte" \ a neighborhood of southern México City

"Café con leche" \ coffee with milk

"caldo de hongos" \ mushroom broth

"cazuelas de barro" \ clay pots

"chocolate caliente" \ hot chocolate

"Coatlicue" \ She of the serpent skirt, legendary mother of Coyolxauhqui

"Concheros" \ a dancer who plays a stringed instrument made from an armadillo shell

"Cuauhtémoc" \ 'Falling Eagle', lord of Tenochtitlán

"Cuitláhuac" \ lord of Tenochtitlán, who was the eleventh son of the ruler Axayacatl

"el arbol de la noche triste" \ the tree of the sad night where Cortéz cried

"el norte" \ the north

"Ese!" \ hey you

"Familia" \ family

"Huitzilopochtli" \ the supreme god of Tenochtitlán, patron of war, fire and the sun

"Huracán Ramírez \ a famous lucha libre wrestler

"Iztaccihuatl" \ the sleeping white woman

"jarras" \ pitchers

"La línea" \ the border line

"La manda" \ pay back for the favors received after praying to the Virgin for her help

"la migra" \ slang for U.S. Immigration and Customs Enforcement

"limpias" \ spiritual cleansing done by a shaman

"más vale tarde que nunca" \ better late than never

"Mestizo" \ a person of mixed blood

"Metztli" \ lowly god who failed to sacrifice himself and became the moon instead

"Mexicatiahui" \ move forward Mexica people, pronounced: Meshica

"milagritos" \ bronze icons shaped in the form of the favor to be requested to the saints

"milongas" \ form of music that preceded the tango

"Nezahualcóyotl" \ 'Fasting Coyote', architect, poet and expert of divine things

"milagros" \ miracles

"mi tierra" \ my land, my country

"mole" \ a spicy sauce made with dry peppers, chocolate and many other ingredients

"Moros y Cristianos" \ Moors and Christians, also a type of Cuban dish of black beans and rice

"Otomí" \ indigenous ethnic group inhabiting the central high planes of México

"Papa Dobles" \ also known as 'Hemingway Daiquiri'

"papel de estraza" \ brown or pink colored wrapping paper

"paramahamsas" \ the topmost class of God-realized devotees in Hinduism

"paso del norte" \ border crossing in El Paso, Texas

"pensamientos" \ thoughts

"Popocatepetl" \ the smoking mountain

"por nuestra raza" \ for our people

"pulque" \ intoxicating beverage brewed from maguey plants

"Purepecha" \ also known as Tarascans, indigenous people from the state of Michoacán

"Quetzalcóatl" \ Feathered serpent—creator god and patron of rulership

"Raza de Bronce" \ Race of Bronze

"rebozo" \ a woman's shawl, popularized by Frida Kahlo

"Reyes Magos y dulces" \ The Three Wise Men
   and sweets

"rudos" \ the rude team, a term used in Lucha Libre
   opposite to the Técnicos

"Tenochtitlán" \ Where México City was founded

"Teponaztle" \ Aztec 'huehuetl' or hollowed wood
   percussion drum

"Tlaloc" \ the great and ancient provider, god of
   rain, fertility and lightning

"Tlaltécatl" \ a man of the earth

"Tonantzin" \ a mother goddess

"Xochipilli" \ god of festivities, song and dance

"y su esperanza"\ and their hope

About the Author

Raúl Sánchez is a Seattle Bio-Tech technician, eschatologist, colletic, prosody enthusiast, hamartiologist, translator, DJ, and cook who conducts workshops on The Day of the Dead. His most recent work is the translation of John Burgess' Punk Poems in his book *Graffito*. He has been a board member of the Washington Poets Association and is a moderator for the Poets Responding to SB 1070 Facebook page.

Raúl comes from a place south where the sun shines fiercely. He lives in a place surrounded by asphalt, cement, full of rushing cars, coffee houses, fancy houses, empty houses. Where seasons shine and hide in the winter months. Where birds stop on their way south to the land of the sun. Where blessed rain, oh! blessed rain falls.

Made in the USA
Lexington, KY
01 September 2018